NUMBER CRUNCHERS

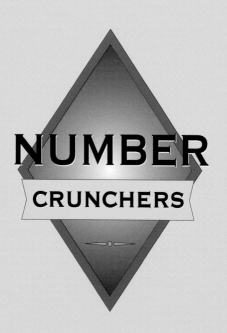

NUMBER
CRUNCHERS

Devised by
David J. Bodycombe

BARNES
&NOBLE
BOOKS
NEW YORK

2004 Barnes & Noble Books

ISBN 0 7607 5469 1

Printed and bound in Singapore

04 05 06 07 08 09 M 9 8 7 6 5 4 3 2 1

INTRODUCTION

Tell people that you devise puzzles for a living and you'll usually get the same response: 'Ugh, I was never any good at mathematics at school.' This is a sad state of affairs when you consider that pretty much the entire world is based on numbers in some form or other, and yet it's a subject that's often neglected.

Part of the reason for this, I feel, is that numbers are rarely placed in an interesting context. Teachers seem to concentrate on finding angles in triangles with barely a mention of how that activity is crucial in civil engineering to keep all manner of different constructions standing, for instance.

One of the aims of this book, therefore, is to offer a varied challenge that pleases the mind as much as the eye. In the pages herein you'll be looking at election results, foreign exchange, international espionage and much more. As well as the subject matter, the difficulty varies throughout the book to keep you on your toes. Some are fairly straightforward, and I guarantee a handful will have you rubbing your eyes with amazement. Sometimes the world of numbers is too strange for words...

And for those of you new to my little patch of the puzzle kingdom, be aware that occasionally there are hidden potholes underfoot. So, if a certain enigma is proving more difficult than you might imagine, chances are you've missed a trick or two.

So grab a pencil, the back of an envelope and your wits and count how many of the following 100 number crunchers you can grind through.

David J. Bodycombe

Jack and Jill played a competitive game several times, betting one pebble on the outcome each time. Jack won seven pebbles, while Jill won seven times. There were no ties.

How many times did they play?

Mary has just opened up a new ice cream stall in the city park. Currently, it takes 4 minutes and 17 seconds for Mary to make a typical ice cream sundae.

Supposing she worked at the same rate throughout, how long would she need to prepare a total of 60 sundaes? See if you can do this without using a calculator.

Each lettered disc hides a number. Any three consecutive discs add up to 16.

What is the value of F?

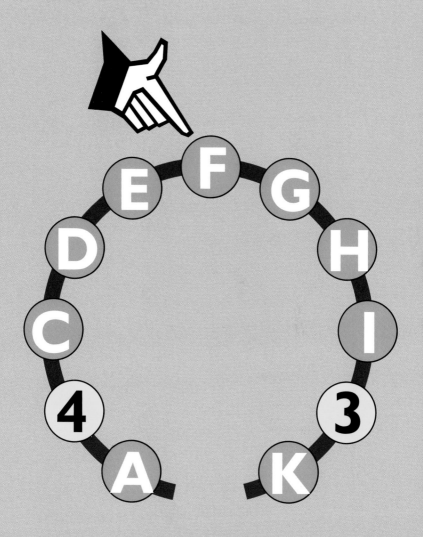

Which three numbers have been jumbled up here?

HIT OFF
ENTIRETY

Egor was to be paid 100 groats plus a shiny new buckle if he worked for Lord Xerxes for one year.

However, Egor had to leave after only seven months so he received fair payment of 20 groats plus the buckle.

How much is the buckle worth?

(a) Place a different number from 1 to 10 in each circle. Each yellow circle must contain the (positive) difference of the two circles it rests upon.

(b) Got the hang of that? OK, now try the same thing for this diagram. This time you'll need to use all the numbers from 1 to 15.

Six spies are stationed in various isolated parts of the world. Each one thinks of a code name for themselves. Each spy needs to know all six code names. When two spies exchange messages, they include all the code names that they know.

How many coded messages do they need to exchange so that every spy knows the code name of every other spy?

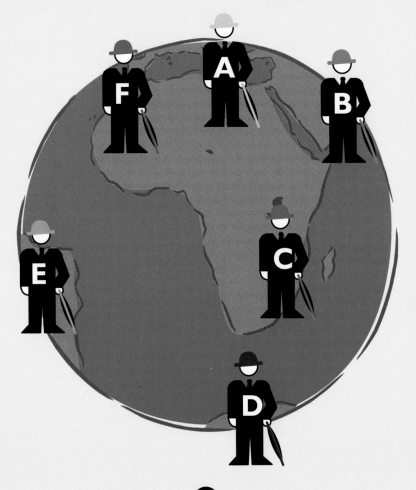

Apart from wanting a serious caffeine hit, why might a mathematician use the following phrase?

Suppose you had a typical gaming die but all the spots were magnetic. You can rearrange the spots as you see fit, but you cannot remove any nor add some extras.

In an experiment, you roll the new die under fair conditions a large number of times. How would your spot rearrangement change the die's average (mean) score?

Little Jimmy hasn't brought his calculator to school. How can he find the value of the expression below just using his own brain power?

$$\frac{67^2 - 33^2}{51^2 - 49^2}$$

The cost of the drink is $2 more than the bottle itself (which is refundable). Therefore, how many bottles of this drink can you buy for $108?

The garden path of Puzzleton Mansions is numbered in a curious way. Each stepping stone (from the third stage onwards) is the sum of the previous two numbers.

What were the original numbers that started the series?

In a standard game of darts, you need to score 501 points finishing on one of the doubles or the bullseye (worth 50 points). It is possible to complete a game using nine darts.

What is the lowest possible number of treble 20s you would need to score during a perfect nine-dart 501 finish?

Place the digits from 1 to 9 into this network, a different digit in every circle. Here's the catch – each pair of connected circles must have a difference of greater than 2. So, for example, 5 can't be in an circle that's connected to 7.

We've started you off.

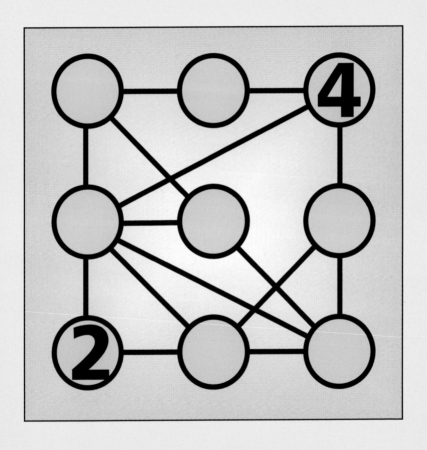

Explain this equation:

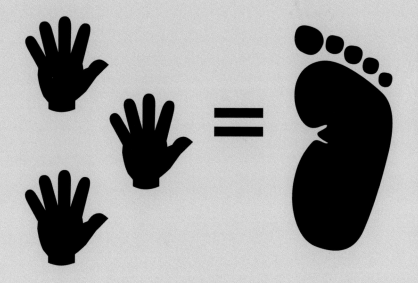

Uh-oh, Gregory Snail is late for work. That's the third time this week, so he better get a move on.

Which method is better: sprint at 3mph for half the journey then drop to 1mph for the rest, or maintain a steady 2mph? Or doesn't it matter?

Be warned: the answer to this will surprise you!

What percentage of whole numbers contain the digit '3'?

The mystical 'biorhythms' are three cycles of 23, 28 and 33 days, each one relating to your Physical, Emotional or Mental well-being.

Suppose these cycles were plotted on a graph, as shown. What calculation would tell you how long it will be before your graph starts to repeat?

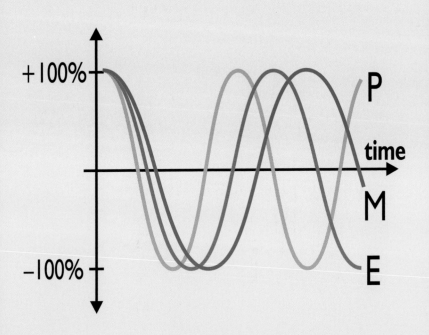

It's sales time at Snazzy Couture and everything must go. Curiously, you find two identical jackets with differing price tags. Ever the opportunist, you decide to work out which one is the bigger bargain. Unfortunately, you don't have any form of calculator handy.

Which one would you choose?

€75

€23

23% OFF!

75% OFF!

See how quickly you can work this out: how many spots are there in total on a complete set of dominoes? Here we're using a standard Western set where the highest number used is 6 spots.

How can you do it using mental arithmetic only?

Write a number in the circle so that, when your chosen number is divided into each of the other numbers, there are no remainders.

The answer is not 1 nor −1.

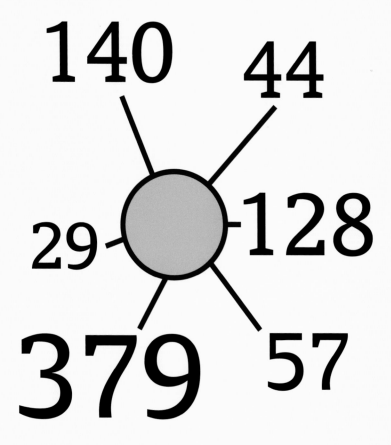

Mr Wolf is always on the lookout for a cunning gamble. While idly tossing a coin, he wondered about this conundrum: True or false – the more times you flip a coin, the greater the probability that the total number of Heads spun equals the number of Tails spun?

In other words, the more times Mr Wolf flips the coin, the more likely that the results will average out to exactly 50-50.

Professor Muddleup dropped his 'pocket' calculator on the hard laboratory floor and – oh, dear – the '0' digit is broken.

(a) How can the professor multiply together two whole numbers so that they result in the product of 1,000,000? Remember, neither number can contain a zero.

(b) Suppose the Professor had to write down **any** two numbers that, when multiplied together, resulted in 1,000,000 except that he had to use the least number of different digits. What would the best solution be?

These four London commuters keep borrowing money from each other to pay for travel tickets and morning coffee. The situation has got so out of hand that they have wound up in a complex web of debts, as illustrated.

What is the **simplest** way for them to settle up?

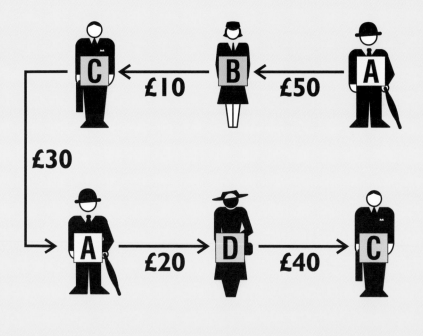

This clock has fallen on the floor, and unfortunately, there is no indication which way 'up' the clock should hang. However, both hands are pointing **precisely** at the minute marks.

You can now work out what the time is.

What is 1 + 3 multiplied by 4 + 2?

Choose from the options below.

12 13 14 15

16 17 18 19

20 21 22 23

25 26 27

The Featherstonehaugh family are planning a circular pond with a triangular fountain in the middle to adorn their immaculately kept gardens. A plan view of the proposed construction is given below.

Given that the equilateral triangle has sides of 3 units, what is the area of the circle?

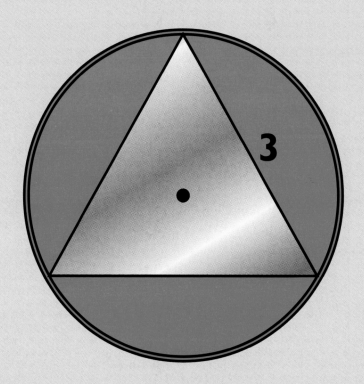

Find the hidden digits:

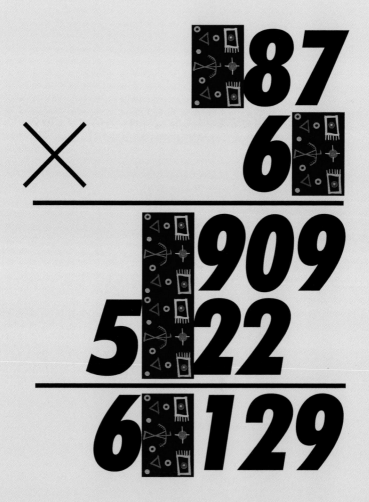

$$
\begin{array}{r}
\blacksquare 87 \\
\times\ 6\blacksquare \\
\hline
\blacksquare 909 \\
5\blacksquare 22 \\
\hline
6\blacksquare 129
\end{array}
$$

The Craddock family have just bought a new jumbo packet of their preferred breakfast cereal, Bran Bombs. A label on the 2kg box reads:

Contains 98% cereal, by total packet weight.

After the first morning, the family have consumed enough cereal than the box now contains 95% cereal by weight.

How much cereal did the family have for breakfast that morning?

Some people say that 0 is not an even number because it is different from the others. A mathematician would always argue that 0 is an even number because it can be divided by 2 without leaving a remainder.

However, there is one well-known exception where 0 is not even. What is it?

In a race, a tortoise and a hare move the number of feet shown on a die that they roll until someone wins.

However, the tortoise only moves on rolls of 1 to 4 (= 1 to 4 feet), and the hare only moves on 5 or 6 (=5 or 6 feet).

Who would you back to win a 1,000ft race?

Think about this: suppose you wanted a number so that, when you multiplied it by seven, the result was a whole string of fours.

What is the smallest number that will do the job?

7 x _____

= 444...4

This is a ziggurat, an ancient Mesopotamian pyramid-shaped tower. It is thought that the Tower of Babel referred to in the Bible was a tower of this kind.

All of the upper six bricks should bear a number equal to the product (multiplication) of the two bricks below it.

Fill in all the numbers given that only whole numbers are used.

Are you the next James Bond? A series of numbers has been found on a microdot, together with a curious diagram.

What code word is being hidden?

Two running partners follow the same route at the same time at the same pace. However, one measures their pace in terms of minutes taken for one mile, whereas the other uses km per hour. Curiously, both statistics turn out to give the same number.

How fast were they going? (Assume 8 km = 5 miles.)

How could you convince a European that this statement was mathematically 'correct'?

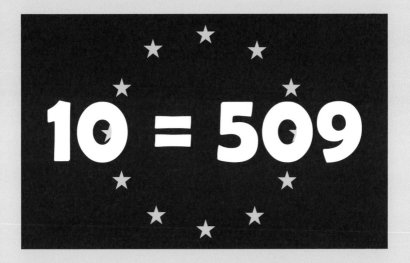

Find two Christian names that you can spell out by writing down two consecutive numbers in each case.

A knock-out soccer tournament for 180 teams is run on the basis that a team is eliminated when they have lost their second match in the competition.

An odd number of matches was played. How many, exactly?

Cut across this ring in three places so that all three sections contain the same total:

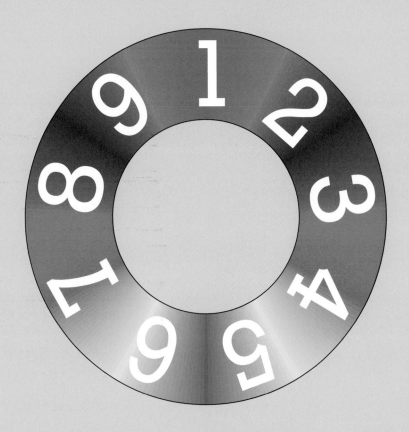

Before being allowed to drive alone, British drivers are tested on their knowledge of the Highway Code. On the back page of the book there is a diagram, similar to the one below, demonstrating the recommended stopping distance for various speeds.

Can you work out the formula that translates miles per hour into overall stopping distance in feet?

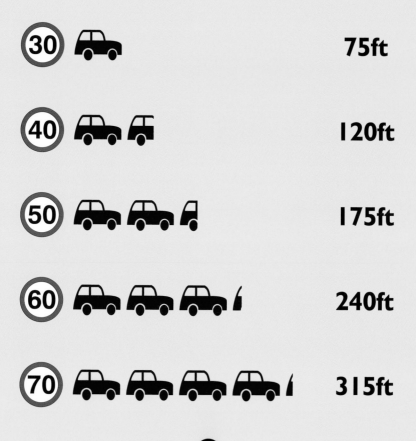

30   75ft

40   120ft

50   175ft

60   240ft

70   315ft

There is a way of expressing the number 1 using all the digits from 0 to 9 exactly once.

We've started it off, can you complete it?

In the baffling Puzzletel, the hotel for brainteaser fans, the rooms are numbered according to how nice they are. The larger the number, the plusher the suite. Unfortunately, they have somewhat complex room numbers.

'Tell you what,' says the bellhop, 'I'll let you choose either room at no extra charge.'

Which room should she pick (i.e. which number is larger)?

Safir went to the camel races with 64 shekels. On each of the six races, he bet half of all the money he currently had on the even money camel (i.e. one shekel paid out for each one shekel bet). Half the camels he backed won, half lost.

Ignoring betting duty, how much did he end up with at the end of the night?

I need to photocopy some notes that I've written on pages 14, 15, 27, 31, 32 and 34 of my pocket notebook.

How much will it cost in total if the charge for one photocopy is 5 pence?

Divide the number 100 up into four parts (call them A, B, C and D) so that adding 4 to A, subtracting 4 from B, dividing C by 4 or multiplying D by 4 gives the same result.

Ernie the electrician can't see very well in his dingy garage. He knows he has 19 fuses of 3 amp rating, 23 fuses of 5 amp rating and 28 fuses of 13 amp rating mixed up in a small dish.

Since the writing on the fuses is too small to see in the poor lighting, how many fuses does he need to take outside in order to be sure of having five fuses of all three ratings?

Out of 100 people surveyed, 20 hadn't touched any reptile before, 67 had touched a snake and 71 had touched a lizard.

How many of those surveyed have touched both a snake and lizard?

While out bowling one evening, Peter notices that there is a large theoretical number of different pin layouts that could remain after the first bowl of a frame has been bowled.

Can you work out the exact number?

Hermanna, the apprentice witch, was taking her wizardry exams. The final question stated:

Q17. This square is magic in that each row, column and main diagonal adds up to the same total.

Although at first she found it difficult, show how Hermanna could complete the question correctly.

Karen had to dash out of her architecture company to pick up her son. However, she needed to work out the area of a crucial washer ring. In a rush, she measured the distance shown.

Later, back at home, she set about calculating the area of the washer in terms of the distance she measured earlier.

How can she do it?

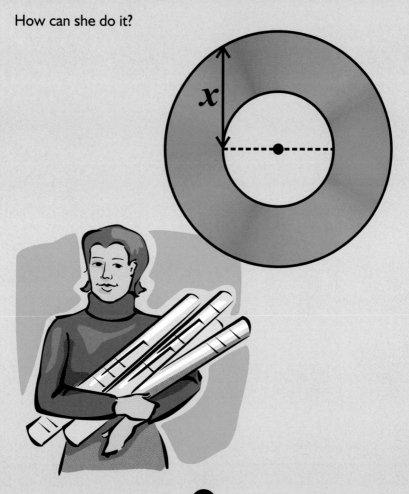

Using only the information supplied in the diagram, determine how far above ground the two wires cross.

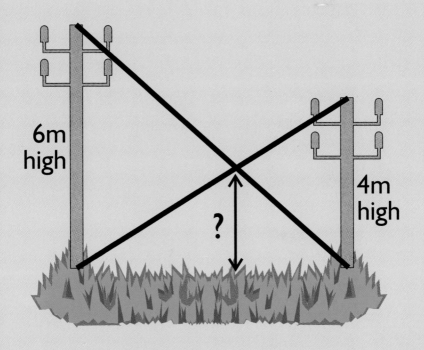

6m high

4m high

?

This lottery scratchcard hides two lemons, one cherry and five 'TRY AGAIN' spaces (which means you can uncover another square for free).

If you uncover the cherry before either lemon, you win.

What are your chances of winning?

Given that this series begins at zero, find the hidden logic.

Then explain why the series can't be continued.

How can the Egyptian god Anubis use his primitive (but accurate) scales three times so that 100g of sand can be split into piles of 82g and 18g?

The problem is he only has 2g and 5g weights.

Dawn was lunching with her seven friends. Everyone opted for the £12 set menu, except for Dawn who spent £3.50 more than the (mean) average.

How much did Dawn's lunch cost?

Move one match so that a valid Roman numeral equation is formed.

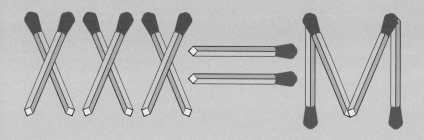

What is the least number of matches you need to move so that this equation is valid?

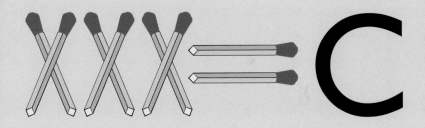

The challenge is to use four different English numbers of five letters in length so that this calculation is correct.

It might seem impossible but some lateral thinking should lead you to a possible solution.

$$(\_\_\_\_\_ \div \_\_\_\_\_)$$

$$+ \_\_\_\_\_$$

$$= \_\_\_\_\_$$

Things were so much easier in the days before the Dotcom crash. At the end of 1999, stonkingrich.com was worth $15 million more than filthylucre.com, $7 million more than goldengoose.com, $12 million more than quids-in.com, and all four were worth $154 million in total.

What was each venture worth?

A golfer was three shots over par at the end of the first day's play. His score on the second day was ten shots better than the first.

What was his score at the end of the second day?

Professor Argy was looking at this diagram one day and asserted that the sphere and the cylinder have the same surface area. Professor Bargy thinks the cylinder has 50% more area.

In fact, they can both be right. How?

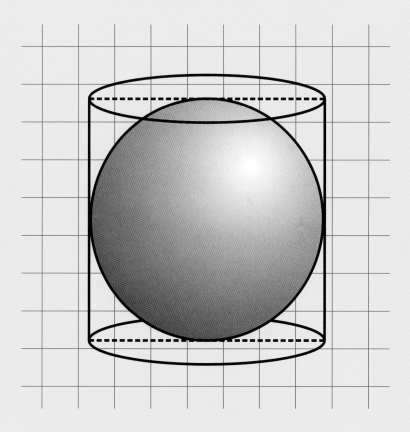

Write a squared number in the square and a cubed number in the cube so that the equation is correct.

Once you've done that, find *another* solution!

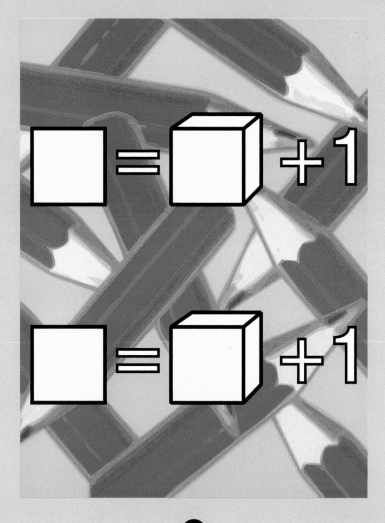

Fran found this curious statement on her husband's typewriter. First work out what he was typing up, then figure out the exact events that led to this result.

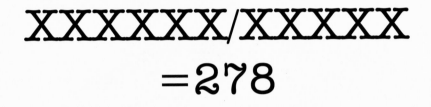

$$XXXXXX/XXXXX =278$$

A car salesman was totting up his turnover for the day. He's been doing a roaring trade, with eight cars sold today alone. He managed to add up all eight figures in his head within 30 seconds without using any calculating device.

Can you?

$94216
$24879
$38255
$15297
$84703
$61745
$75121
+ $ 5784

After a pleasant trip to Switzerland, I have a certain amount of money in my wallet. The number of centimes is treble plus one of the number of whole francs.

Alternatively, if you were to swap the centime and franc figures, the result would be treble plus one centime more than what I actually have.

How much money is in my wallet? (100 centimes = 1 franc)

Derek Boost, personal fitness trainer to the stars, always carries around a water cylinder (shown on the left) to rehydrate himself. The cylinder can hold one pint of water.

Unfortunately, one day Derek manages to leave the plastic cylinder out in the strong sun. When he finds it, he discovers that it is somewhat out of shape. Although largely intact, the cylinder has the same base area but is now slanted by 30 degrees (as shown on the right).

Assuming it is still watertight, what is the current capacity of Derek's water cylinder?

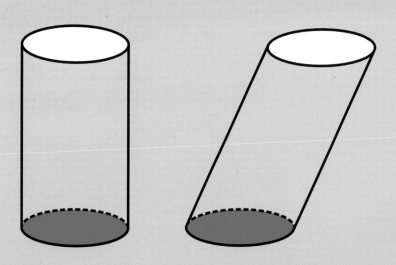

A standard cricket team has eleven players. If the ninth batsman of one team has just gone in to bat, how many wickets must fall before that team is out?

Be warned, you'll really need to think about this one.

The puzzle is to rearrange the symbols in this equation *as little as possible* so that it is now correct.

Do you know the trick?

$$(11 + 1) \times (11 - 1) = 51.$$

A six-sided gaming die has non-standard numbering. If the die was to be rolled twice, the six possible total scores are shown below.

(a) Given that each side bears a whole number, how many different numbers appear on the die?

(b) If 4, 6 and 12 is half as likely as 5, 8 and 9, identify all six sides on the die.

Timmy was doing his maths homework and – ugh – it was his nemesis: fractions.

'That's not the way to simplify fractions,' nagged his sister. 'Hang on, you've still got the correct answer... somehow!'

Can you identify which fundamental mathematical law Timmy broke (inadvertently) yet still obtained the correct answer?

$$\frac{16}{64}$$

$$\frac{26}{65}$$

$$\frac{19}{95}$$

$$\frac{49}{98}$$

Complete this magic square such that:

(a) it contains nine consecutive numbers, and

(b) each row, column and main diagonal totals the same.

Grunthilda is going shopping in the village. She offers to pay for €7 of goods with a €20 note, and yet the shop keeper asks if she has a €50 note.

Why might this possibly happen?

The ____ of a 50% possibility is ____.

You are at a party with nine other people. When you leave, you ask everyone how many people they've shaken hands with at the party. The answers you get are '1', '2', '3', etc. up to '9'. In other words, everyone's shaken hands with a different number of people.

How many people have you shaken hands with at the party?

In a 'round robin' baseball tournament, 13 teams play everyone else once. Winning a match earns $100. Tied matches earn $50 for each team.

How much prize money will be given out during this tournament?

Horace Grimwold works in the Ministry of Statistics. It is his job to look after all the measurable statistics in the world such as mountain heights, unemployment statistics, river lengths, country populations and so on.

Due to a department underspend, Horace is given the task of reordering all the numbers in the department according to their initial digit. So, for example, if 726,193 people live in a certain city, that would be spiked on to pin number '7'.

Curiously, as the statistics mounted up on their respective piles, Horace found that approximately 30% of the numbers in the overall list begin with what digit?

Also, if Horace put his nine spikes of statistics in a row, what overall shape will the piles take?

Which two symbols should be placed in the blank squares to complete the logical progression?

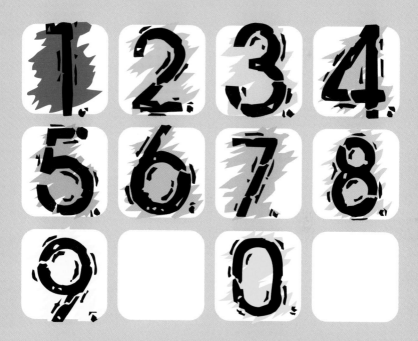

For Christmas, I was given a handy gadget that enables you to take small leftover pieces from bars of soap and compress them together to form an entire new bar. Six leftover pieces form one new bar.

As it happens, I have been saving up 246 soap leftovers for just this purpose. How many bars of soap am I going to get for free?

There is a way in which you can take the numbers from one to ten and arrange them into a palindrome – in other words, the sequence reads the same whether read from left to right or right to left. This is shown below.

In what way is this series a 'palindrome'?

1 4 3 5 10 2 6 9 8 7

Sir Prancealot earns two groats if he guards the castle for the day, but forfeits three groats if he goes outside for some fresh air instead.

Over the last 30 days, his earnings have been zero on aggregate. How many days did he work?

In Natasha's secret sweets drawer, all but three bars are licorice, all but three bars are pure chocolate, and all but three bars are pure toffee.

How many bars of candy does Natasha have stashed in her drawer?

(a) You are offered two amounts of money. Which one would you prefer?

(b) In the general case, under what conditions does this hold true? In other words, what correlation does there have to be between A and B for the equation to work?

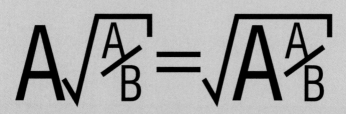

Mr Strangely is enjoying his current hobby of choice, rolling down a 64-yard hill in a barrel.

In time terms, how far is he through his journey to the bottom of the hill when he is 16 yards down the slope?

Two regular dice are placed face-to-face so that one side (chosen at random) is made to touch the same numbered side on the other die.

If this procedure was repeated many times, what is the average (mean) number of spots that would touch face-to-face each time?

The final 'check' digit of an ISBN number is found by taking each of the previous digits and multiplying them by 1, 2, 3... up to 9 respectively, totalling this up, then taking the remainder after division by 11.

Using the ISBN below as an example:

(0x1) + (7x2) + (6x3) + (0x4) + (7x5) + (5x6) + (4x7) + (6x8) + (9x9)

= 14 + 18 + 35 + 30 + 28 + 48 + 81 = 254.

254/11 = 23 remainder 1, so 1 is the check digit.

(a) Why is this multiplication system used, rather than (e.g.) simply adding the digits?

(b) What happens if the remainder is 10?

ISBN 0-7607-5469-1

Two-thirds of an odd number gives you an even result if the starting number is divisible by 3 (see example).

Two-thirds of which odd number gives an even result even though it is not a multiple of 3?

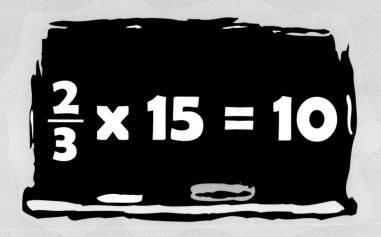

$$\frac{2}{3} \times 15 = 10$$

ST ND RD TH TH TH TH TH TH TH

TH TH TH TH TH

TH TH TH TH TH

??

A number is hidden inside each cube. To give you a chance at discovering them, someone has stamped a number on the top of each cube. This number shows you the total of the numbers inside the boxes connected to it (not including the box on which the number is printed).

What number is in each cube?

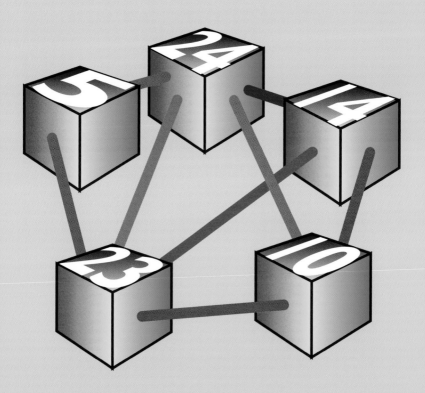

A farmer has been busy at work in his triangular plot of land (XYZ). There is only a small amount of land left to plow, denoted by triangle PQZ.

P is two-thirds of the way down the XZ line, and Q is three-quarters of the way down the XY line.

If the whole of the farmer's land has an area of 20 acres, what is the area of PQZ?

At the weekend, Mary usually cuts her grass lawn in 4 hours. However, today she has Mungo to help her.

If, with Mungo's constant help, the job now took 2 hours 24 minutes, how long would it take Mungo to mow the lawn on his own?

During a charity telethon broadcast by a local Scottish TV channel, three digits fell out of their scoreboard showing how much money they had currently raised.

What is the chance that the original number was divisible by 18? Starting hint: there are six ways to arrange three digits.

TOTAL SO FAR
£15☐,9☐☐

Here are the election results hot off the press.

If these figures were rounded to the nearest one per cent, what is the lowest possible value for X?

Ivor Seat	28%
Sue Near	22%
Linda Middle	21%
Peter Out	17%
Others	X%

What should the final arrow contain?

Here's a puzzle with a twist. If you removed two of the digital segments and moved two others, which familiar series could you form?

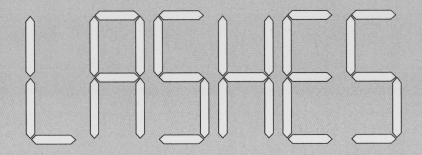

What is unusual about the results of these equations?

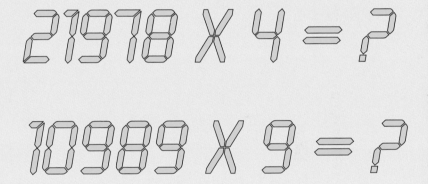

What does this dot-to-dot form?

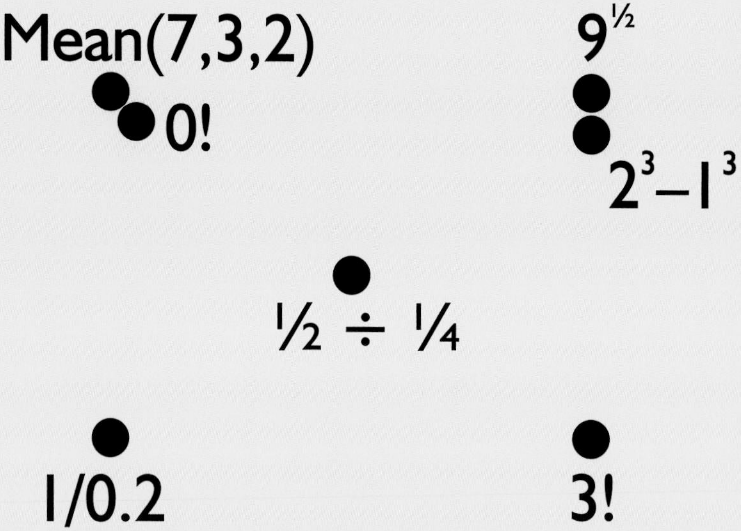

Mean(7,3,2)

$0!$

$9^{1/2}$

$2^{3}-1^{3}$

$1/2 \div 1/4$

$1/0.2$

$3!$

Suppose there was a limit placed on the number and types of stamps you could stick to an air mail letter.

(a) If you were allowed to stick a maximum of three stamps on a letter, which three denominations of stamps would you choose to allow you to post any letter from 1 to 15 cents?

(b) If the three stamp limit was still in force but you were now allowed to choose from four different denominations, how could you create any value of stamps from 1 to 24 cents?

This system doesn't look like it should balance, but it does. Can you think of a likely explanation?

(Assume weight of rods/hooks=0)

Which positive whole number is equal to triple the sum of its digits? Surprisingly, there is only one possible answer.

If you reverse the digits in Deborah's age, you obtain her grandfather's age. As it happens, his birthday is tomorrow, when his age will become twice Susan's.

Find both their ages.

ANSWERS

ANSWERS TO PUZZLES ENDING IN −1

1 If Jack is up seven pebbles, that means he's won seven times more than he's lost. He lost seven times, since Jill won seven times. Hence, Jack won 7 + 7 = 14 times.

Games played
= Jack's wins + Jill's wins
= 14 + 7 = 21.

11 The trick is to notice that you can buy more drinks by refunding your empty bottles. The drink costs $2.50, and the bottle refund is 50 cents.

Initially, you can buy 36 drinks which creates 36 returnable bottles. This buys you (36x0.50)/$3 = 6 more drinks, which creates another six empty bottles. This can buy you one final drink. So in total you can obtain 36+6+1=43 drinks.

21 A fraction such as ½ would do. Dividing by ½ is the same as doubling the

number, so there would be no remainders.

31 Tortoise's average roll
= (1+2+3+4)/4 = 2.5ft.

Hare's average roll
= (5+6)/2=5.5ft.

Although the tortoise wins twice as many rolls, its average move is less than half that of the hare.

Therefore, over the long term the hare will win (for a change).

41
$$\frac{35}{70} + \frac{148}{296} = 1$$

It looks scary until you notice that it's just a long-winded way of writing ½ + ½ = 1.

51 Either solve this graphically using y=4x and y=−6x+6 then solve for x and y, or directly via: (6x4)/(6+4) = 24/10 = 2.4m. Curiously, this doesn't depend on the distance between the poles.

61 The area of a sphere is equal to $4 \times \pi \times radius^2$.

The curved part of the cylinder is equal to the circumference of one edge multiplied by the height, or $(2 \times \pi \times r) \times (2 \times r)$ which equals $4\pi r^2$ – i.e. the same.

However, you could interpret the diagram as being a closed cylinder, with capped ends at the top and bottom. You would then need to add the area of two circles on to the total. This gives:

$$(4\pi r^2) + 2 \times (\pi r^2)$$
$$= 6\pi r^2$$

This has increased the area by 50%, as claimed by Professor Bargy.

71 Each line totals 9:

81 4½ bars (1½ of each variety).

91 Note that $18 = 2 \times 9$, so the number needs to be divisible by 2 and 9. Also note that one digit could be '6' or '9':

If '6', the total of the digits = 33, which (by a well-known rule) means that the number cannot be divisible by 9 for any of the 6 possible combinations.

If '9', the number will be divisible by 9, and divisible by 2 only if the 9 isn't the last digit – that accounts for 4 of those 6 possibilities.

Therefore, the chance that the number can be divided by 18 is 4/12, or 1/3.

ANSWERS TO PUZZLES ENDING IN –2

2 4 hours and 17 minutes. When multiplying by 60, the minutes become hours and the seconds become minutes.

12 Let the first numbers be A and B. The third number will therefore be A+B, the fourth A+2B, and so 2A+3B=19. Continue like this to get 8A+13B=81.

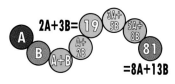

Multiplying 2A+3B=19 by 4 gives 8A+12B=76. Subtracting this from the second equation gives B=81–76=5, and hence A=2.

22 Believe it or not, it's false. The chance of equal Heads and Tails after two spins is ½. After four spins, it's ½ x ¾ = 3/8. After 6 spins it's ½ x ¾ x 5/6 = 5/16.

You can probably predict the trend. The number gets smaller the more you spin.

If you think about it, that makes sense because after N spins there are N+1 possible totals of which only one has equal numbers of Heads and Tails.

32 If N x 7 = 4...4, then N = 4...4 / 7. So the trick is to divide 7 into a string of 4s until you get no remainder:

$$7\overline{)444444444...}$$ = 63492

7 into 44 gives 6 rem 2
7 into 24 gives 3 rem 3
7 into 34 gives 4 rem 6
7 into 64 gives 9 rem 1
7 into 14 gives 2 exactly

So, 7 x 63492 = 444444.

42 With equations, you can usually do what you like as long as you do it to either side, particularly if both numbers are positive. e.g. there is no reason why we can't square both sides.

In fact, if we raise both sides to the 15th power the puzzle becomes very easy:

$$\left(10^{\frac{1}{5}}\right)^{15} = 10^3$$

$$\left(4^{\frac{1}{3}}\right)^{15} = 4^5$$

$10^3 = 1000$ whereas $4^5 = 1024$.

So the right-hand suite is going to be the better choice as it has a larger room number.

52 1-in-3, since the chance that the first fruit you uncover is a cherry is 1/3. It's as simple as that. The TRY AGAIN spaces are, effectively, a distraction.

62 (a) 9 and 8 – i.e. 3 squared and 2 cubed.

(b) 0 squared = (−1) cubed + 1.

72 If the shop keeper had no €5 or €10 notes, giving €3 in coins and two €20 notes (in return for €50) is favourable to giving €13 in coins (in return for €20).

82 We'll do part (b) first. Squaring both sides gives:

$A^2 \times (A/B) = A + (A/B)$. So $A^3 = (A \times B) + A$ or, simplifying, $A^2 = B + 1$.

We can now see that the numbers in part (a) are equal since $3 \times 3 = 8 + 1$.

92 10%. Even though this gives a total of only 98% for the numbers in the table, this is still possible due to rounding-down error (e.g. the results might have been 28.4, 22.4, 21.4, 17.4, 10.4).

ANSWERS TO PUZZLES ENDING IN –3

3 Note that if $4+C+D=16$ and $C+D+E=16$, then $E=4$. By a similar argument on the other side, $G=3$. $16=E+F+G=4+F+3$, so $F=9$.

13 It's possible with only three treble 20s, followed by five treble 19s and ending with double 18 (alternative routes are possible).

23 (a) The prime factors of 1,000,000 are 2, 2, 2, 2, 2, 2, 5, 5, 5, 5, 5 and 5. Whenever you combine a 2 and a 5, you'll get a figure ending in 10. We don't want that, so we have to keep the 2s and 5s apart. Hence, the two numbers are:

$2\times2\times2\times2\times2\times2=2^6=64$, and
$5\times5\times5\times5\times5\times5=5^6=15,625$.

(b) Technically, you could use the '9' as follows: $999.999... \times 999.999... = 1,000,000$. Mathematically, $999.999... = 1,000$.

33

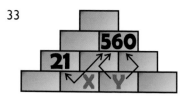

The only way you can form 21 is 7 x 3 (prime factors). Likewise, $560 = 2 \times 2 \times 2 \times 2 \times 5 \times 7$.

They have to share a factor in common (see position X in diagram), so that has to be the '7'.

Whichever factor goes in position Y will contribute to 560 twice. There is only one factor of 5 but, in effect, two lots of 4 (2 x 2).

So, we can now fill in the rest of the ziggurat:

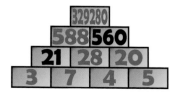

43 Suppose he lost the first three races then won the next three. The results would be as follows:

Race 1: Lose 32 (32 left)
Race 2: Lose 16 (16 left)
Race 3: Lose 8 (8 left)
Race 4: Win 4 (12 left)
Race 5: Win 6 (18 left)
Race 6: Win 9 (27 left)

Safir would end up with 27 shekels. Strangely, it doesn't actually matter which exact races he won and lost – the result's always the same.

53 The last letter gives the first letter of the next highest whole number: zerO, OnE, EighT, TeN, NineteeN, NinetY. There are no numbers beginning with Y.

63 For once it's nothing to do with Roman numerals. In fact, Fran's husband was typing up some tenpin bowling scores from his game the previous night.

There were 11 strikes (denoted by X) and one spare (denoted by /).

With one spare in the frame, any score from 270 to 279 could be possible. To achieve 278 exactly, the first ball in the seventh frame knocked down eight pins, and the remaining two pins were cleared up by the second.

73 The ODDS of a 50% possibility is EVENS (i.e. an 'even money' probability is a 50-50 bet).

83 He is halfway through his journey. This is because in the distance down the hill is proportional to the square of the time taken. Hence, 16 yards = 4 time units, whereas 64 yards = 8 time units.

93 The first five arrows are pointing to the bearings of **Z**ero, **F**ifteen, **T**hirty, **S**ixty and **N**inety degrees.

Therefore, the final arrow should contain OHAE for One Hundred and Eighty.

ANSWERS TO PUZZLES ENDING IN –4

4   In the phrase HIT OFF ENTIRETY, you will find the letters for THIRTEEN, FIFTY and O (zero).

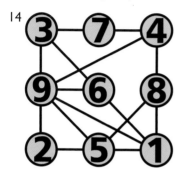

24 Mr A owes £50 + £20 and is owed £30, so he must repay £40 to be even. Similarly, Miss B is owed £40 net (10 – 50), Mr C is owed £20 net (10 – 30 + 40) and Mrs D owes £20 net (20 – 40).

Hence, two transactions are needed – Mr A should give Miss B £40, and Mrs D should give £20 to Mr C.

34 Note that 47 = 1 + 2 + 4 + 8 + 32. Shading in those segments on the diagram gives an 'H'.

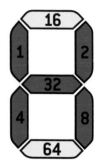

Similarly, 95 = O, 55 = P and so on. If you complete this for each number you spell out HOPEFUL.

44 25 pence – because it's a small notebook, the spread covering pages 14 and 15 can fit on to one copy. Note that page 31 is on the back of page 32, so the same trick doesn't work then.

54 Here's the sneaky bit: take all the sand and divide it evenly so that there is 50g of sand on each pan. Now take one of those piles and repeat the process to give 25g of sand on each pan.

Finally, place both weights

on one pan and weigh out
7g (5+2) as normal from
one of your 25g piles.

50+25+7=82g. Whatever
sand remains = 18g. (Can
you find another method?)

64 Note that the 1st & 8th,
2nd & 7th, 3rd & 6th and
4th & 5th numbers total
$100,000. Hence, the grand
total = $400,000.

74 Five. For brevity, let the
person who met X people
be called 'Mr X'. Mr 1 must
have met Mr 9 (who met
everyone); Mr 2 must
therefore have met Mr 8
(who met everyone except
Mr 1) and Mr 9. By pairing
off 1 & 9, 2 & 8, 3 & 7 and 4
& 6, you're left with Mr 5.
So you must have met five
people too.

84 Care is necessary because
some combinations of faces
have two different possible
orientations. For example, a
2 against a 2 could have two
or zero touching dots:

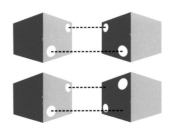

Similarly, 3 against 3 could
have 1 or 3 spots matching,
and 6 against 6 could have 4
or 6 spots matching.

Therefore, average is:
[1 + (avg. of 0 & 2)
+ (avg. of 1 & 3)+ 4 + 5
+ (avg. of 4 & 6)] /6

= 18/6 = 3.

94 You can form the numbers
from 2 to 7 (but you need
to twist the page upside-
down first!)

ANSWERS TO PUZZLES ENDING IN –5

5 If the buckle is worth X groats, then
$(7/12) \times (100 + X)$
$= 20 + X$, hence
$700 + 7X = 240 + 12X$.
This simplifies to $5X = 460$, so $X = 92$.

15 One hand, a measurement used to measure horses, is a distance of four inches. Hence, three hands = 3×4 = 12 inches = 1 foot.

25 From midnight (or noon), the number of minutes that have passed must be a multiple of 12 because that is the only time that the hour hand points to one of the 'ticks' exactly.

It turns out that the only possibility for the hands to be in the required position occurs at 2:12.

35 M minutes per mile is the same as $(60/M)$mph
$= (60 \times 1.6/M)$km/h
$= 96/M$ km/h

By the question, this equals M km/h. In other words, $96 / M = M$, so M is the square root of 96 (approximately 9.8).

45 Let 'x' be the result we get each time. Then $A = x–4$, $B = x+4$, $C = 4x$ and $D = x/4$.

Adding these together:
$100 = A + B + C + D$
$= (x–4)+(x+4)+4x+(x/4)$
$= 6x + \frac{1}{4}x = 25x/4$.

If $100 = 25x/4$, then $x = 400/25 = 16$. Putting this back into our original equations, we obtain:
$A = 12$, $B = 20$, $C = 64$, $D = 4$.

55 Let the average = A.

A = Total cost divided by total number of diners
$= (7 \times 12 + (A + 3.5))/8$.

$7A = 87.5$, so $A = £12.50$.

Therefore, Dawn's meal cost £16.

65 Let F be the number of whole francs. We can then express the number of centimes as $3F+1$. We are told that swapping the figures triples the total and adds an extra centime. Hence, (3F+1 francs and F centimes) equals 3 x (F francs and 3F+1 centimes) plus one centime.

Convert this to centimes throughout:
$100x(3F+1) + F$
$= 3x(100F + 3F + 1) + 1.$

This simplifies to:
$301F + 100 = 309F + 4$
$8F = 96$, hence $F = 12$.

Therefore, I had 12 francs and $(3x12+1) = 37$ centimes in my wallet.

75 There will be $\frac{1}{2}$ x (13 x 12) = 78 matches with $100 given out for each match regardless of the outcome, so the total will be $7,800.

85 (a) The idea is that sometimes people enter the correct digits but the wrong way around when typing on a computer, for example. If two digits are transposed, the check digit will usually

be different enabling a computer to tell whether a valid number has been entered. This detection system wouldn't work if the mathematical calculation was more straightforward.

(b) An X is used as the check digit. You may have seen this on other books.

95 The answers are 87912 and 98901 respectively, i.e. the reverse of the first term of the multiplication.

ANSWERS TO PUZZLES
ENDING IN –6

6 (a)

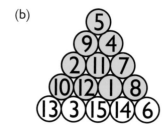

(b)

16 Time = distance/speed. Let
    is say that the distance is
    equal to 2d.

    Option 1:
    Time = d/3 + d/1 =
    (4/3)d.

    Option 2:
    Time = 2d/2 = d

    Hence, option 2 (a steady
    speed) is quicker.

26 The normal rules of
    arithmetic say you should
    perform multiplication
    before addition. Hence,
    1+(3x4)+2=15.

36 10 in French is DIX.

    509 in Roman numerals is
    DIX.

    Hence, DIX = DIX.

46 If you answered 47, that's
    incorrect. The worst case
    scenario occurs when Ernie
    takes all the 5 amp and 13
    amp fuses first (since there
    are more of these), then 5
    of the 3 amp fuses. The
    total is 23 + 28 + 5 = 56
    fuses.

56 Move one match from the
    second X so that it reads

    A bar over a numeral
    multiplies it by 1000, so the
    statement is equivalent to
    10,000 / 10 = 1000.

66 Believe it or not, the
    capacity is still one pint.
    This is because capacity =
    base area x perpendicular
    height. Since both area and
    height have not changed,
    neither has the volume.

76 Amazingly, 30% of all statistics in the world begin with the digit '1'. This is because measurable items are usually finite, so numbers start with '1' much more often than '9'.

Why? Well, imagine for the moment that all numbers have two digits. In order for a number to begin with a '9', it mustn't stop in the 10s, 20s, 30s, 40s, 50s, 60s, 70 or 80s (i.e. unlikely).

This argument can be repeated for numbers of any length, so overall the piles will stack up something like this:

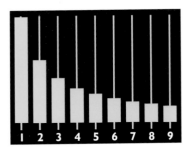

86 Two-thirds of ELEVEN is EVEN!

96 $0! = 1$, $\frac{1}{2} \div \frac{1}{4} = 2$, 9 to power of $\frac{1}{2}$ = sq. root of 9 = 3, Mean(7,3,2) = 4 [mean average], $1/0.2 = 5$, $3! = 6$ and $2^3 - 1^3 = 7$.

Tracing in this order, an envelope is formed:

ANSWERS TO PUZZLES ENDING IN –7

7 Eight messages will be required. One way is A&B, D&E, A&D, C&F, C&D, A&F, E&F and B&C.

17 Believe it or not, 100%. Look at it this way: the likelihood of the number containing a '3' for a one-digit number is 10%. For two digits, this rises to 19%. For three digits, it's 27.1%. Continuing this argument to numbers of infinite length, you would get 100% of numbers containing '3'.

Adding up all these percentages over all lengths of numbers gives you a total of 100% too.

Incidentally, the percentage of numbers containing (or excluding) any given digit is also 100%. Such are the problems of percentages used with infinite sets of numbers.

27 Draw in some extra lines:

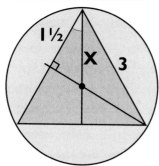

We are trying to find the radius of the circle, X. One way to do this is to notice that the yellow angle must be 30 degrees and use some trigonometry:

$$\cos 30 = 1.5 / X$$
$$X = 1.5 / \cos 30$$
$$= 1.5 / (\sqrt{3}/2) = 3/\sqrt{3}$$
$$= \sqrt{3}$$

Hence, area of circle
$$= \pi \times \text{radius}^2 = \pi \times X^2$$
$$= \pi \times (\sqrt{3})^2 = 3\pi.$$

37 Obviously, you need to use Roman numerals. The names are VIV (6, 5) and LIL (51, 50).

47 Number of people who have touched a snake only must be equal to 100 less 20 less 71 = 9.

Similarly, lizard only = 100 − 20 − 67 = 13.

Hence, people who have touched both = 100 − people who have touched snake only, lizard only or none at all = 100 − 9 − 13 − 20 = 58.

57 None if you consider the second X to be a multiplication sign: 10 x 10 = 100.

67 Many people answer 'two' to this question, but the correct answer is 'three'. Ten wickets need to fall in total for a team to be out, yet only seven players have been judged out at that stage.

77 The symbols * and #, to complete this sequence of keys on a typical telephone keypad.

87 ST as this is the '21st' term. The series is the letters used when writing out abbreviated ordinal numbers (1st, 2nd, 3rd, 4th, 5th...)

97 (a) Choose stamps costing 1, 4 and 5 cents. Every value from 1 to 15 can be made thus:

1 cent: 1
2 cents: 1 + 1
3 cents: 1 + 1 + 1
4 cents: 4
5 cents: 5
6 cents: 5 + 1
7 cents: 5 + 1 + 1
8 cents: 4 + 4
9 cents: 5 + 4
10 cents: 5 + 5
11 cents: 5 + 5 + 1
12 cents: 4 + 4 + 4
13 cents: 5 + 4 + 4
14 cents: 5 + 5 + 4
15 cents: 5 + 5 + 5

(b) Choose stamps of value 1, 4, 7 and 8 cents.

ANSWERS TO PUZZLES ENDING IN –8

8   The letters in each word form a mnemonic (memory jogger) for the first eight digits of pi, which are 3.1415926.

18 Because 23, 28 and 33 do not share any common factors, the calculation is simply 23 x 28 x 33. This is every 21,252 days, or roughly 58 years 66 days. (On reaching this age, one is supposed to experience a moment of 'rebirth'.)

28

$$\begin{array}{r} 987 \\ \times \quad 67 \\ \hline 6909 \\ 5922 \\ \hline 66129 \end{array}$$

38 If everyone had been eliminated, there would have been 360 matches since each match creates one losing team. As there is one winner, there must have been 358 or 359 matches. 359 is an odd number, so that's the answer.

48 When you bowl a ball, each pin will have been knocked down or remains standing. Thus, there are two possible states for each of the ten pins.

Therefore, the number of different possible patterns is 2x2x2x2x2x2x2x2x2x2 or 2 to the power of 10 $= 2^{10} = 1024$.

58 One solution is: (GROSS/DOZEN)+EIGHT = SCORE. This is correct as $(144 \div 12) + 8 = 20$.

68 Note that the left hand side is equal to 120. This is the same as 5x4x3x2x1 which is 5 factorial, written as 5!

So, move the full stop underneath the final 1:

$$(11 + 1) \times (11 - 1) = 5!$$

78 Immediately, I can form 246/6 = 41 bars from the leftovers I currently have. Once I've used those 41 bars, that will create 41 leftovers. This gives me 41/6 = 6 more bars (and 5 unused leftovers). Those 6 bars, once used, will generate one further bar. When I have used that last bar, I am left with one little piece.

Here's the clever bit: I can join this together with the 5 unused leftovers I had from before. This ekes out one extra bar of soap. That's all I can do. In total, I have had the use of 41 + 6 + 1 + 1 = 49 bars for free.

88 The number inside each cube is shown below:

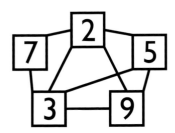

98 The weight that looks like a 9 has been hooked on upside-down. A 6 weight at that position would be exactly right to make the system balance.

Using the formula Moment = Mass x Distance:

Left side: 8x2 + 6 = 22

Right side: 3x2 + 4x4 = 22

Hence, balances.

ANSWERS TO PUZZLES ENDING IN −9

9 It would not change the average at all. There will still be 21 spots on 6 faces, giving an average score of 3.5 – exactly the same as a standard die.

19 In fact, they are both the same. This is because (23/100) x 75 and (75/100) x 23 are the same calculations but written different ways.

29 The packaging must weigh 40g (2% of 2kg) so cereal weighs 1960g. After breakfast, the 40g accounts for 1/20th of the weight.

Total pack weight is now 40 x 20 = 800g, so the family ate 1160g of cereal.

39

49

10	A	B
2	C	D
5	E	F

In a 3x3 magic square, the central number (C in the diagram) is always one-third of the total for any line.

We are given a complete line which totals 17, hence the magic number must be one-third of this which is 17/3. The catch is that we have to use fractions.

It is now simple to work out that B=19/3, D=28/3, and E=32/3. This leaves us with A=2/3 and F=4/3.

59 Let stonkingrich.com's value be represented by X.

X + (X−15) + (X−7) + (X−12) = 154

4X − 34 = 154

4X = 188, so X = 47.

The others are worth $32m, $40m and $35m.

69 (a) Given that there are six different outcomes possible there must be three different numbers on the die. (If there were four, say, then ten outcomes would be possible.) In other words, some numbers are used more than once.

(b) Since 4 is the lowest number possible and 12 is the highest, there must be a 2 and a 6. From here, you can work out that the other number must be a 3. So those are the three different numbers on the die. Since 4, 6 and 12 are equally likely as each other, the numbers on the die must be 2, 2, 3, 3, 6 and 6.

79 If you convert all the numbers to Roman numerals, you get a palindromic result: I IV III V X II VI IX VIII VII.

89 By a theorem, the ratio of XQ:QY is the same as Area XQZ:Area QZY.

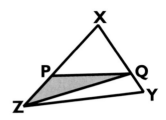

As stated, XQ is ¾ of the way down the line XY. So:

Area of triangle XQZ
= ¾ of total
= ¾ of 20 = 15.

We can now repeat this trick on the left-hand side. The ratio of the lines XP:PY will be the same as Area XQP:Area QPZ.

So, area of PQZ will be 1/3 of 15, so the answer is 5 acres.

99 It's not difficult to deduce that it must be a two-digit number, which we can write as $10a + b$, where a is the tens value and b is the units.

$10a + b = 3(a+b)$, hence $7a = 2b$. The only possibility is a=2, b=7 so the answer is 27.

ANSWERS TO PUZZLES
ENDING IN –0

10 In general terms, $a^2 - b^2$
$= a^2 - ab + ab - b^2$
$= (a–b) \times (a+b)$.

So we can now write the equation much simpler:

$(34 \times 100) / (2 \times 100)$
$= 34 / 2 = 17$.

20 Any given digit (0 to 6) appears once on six dominoes and twice on the double. So the series 0 to 6 (total: 21) is used eight times over, which gives $21 \times 8 = 168$.

30 Placing your money on the EVEN space in roulette does not count as a win if 0 or 00 comes up.

40 In table form:

30	75ft	(2.5x)
40	120ft	(3x)
50	175ft	(3.5x)
60	240ft	(4x)
70	315ft	(4.5x)

The final column shows the multiplier in effect between the speed and the stopping distance.

Working backwards, at 0mph (standstill) the multiplier would be 1x. Each additional 20mph doubles the stopping distance. Hence, the final formula is:

Distance = $X + (X^2/20)$ where X = speed in mph.

50

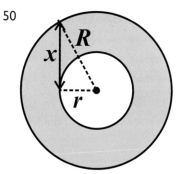

If the larger and smaller circles have radius R and r, then Area = $\pi(R^2 - r^2)$.

Draw in the radius (of length R) from the top of the arrow to the origin.

Using Pythagoras on that right-angled triangle shows that:

$x^2 = R^2 - r^2$, hence
Area $= \pi(R^2 - r^2) = \pi x^2$.

60 If his second round is ten shots better than $+3$, he will be -7 for that round. The cumulative score for both rounds is therefore -7 and $+3$ which is -4 overall. So four under par is the answer.

70 If you 'cancel out' the 6s in 16/64 (something you shouldn't normally do), you are left with 1/4 which does equal 16/64. So it works even though it shouldn't!

Similarly:

$$\frac{26}{65} = \frac{2}{5}$$

$$\frac{49}{98} = \frac{4}{8}$$

$$\frac{19}{95} = \frac{1}{5}$$

80 Suppose the knight works for W days, then holidays for (30–W) days.

2W – 3x(30–W) = 0, so
2W – 90 + 3W = 0.

Rearranging gives 5W = 90, or W=18.

90 Work rate = Area/Time. Suppose lawn is of area A.

Then Mungo's work rate
= Rate of both Mary and Mungo minus Mary's rate
= A/(2.4) – A/4
= 10A/24 – 6A/24
= 4A/24 = A/6.

Hence Mungo would take 6 hours by himself.

100 Let Deborah's two-digit age be 10a+b. Currently, 10b+a = 2(10a+b) – 1, which simplifies to 19a = 8b+1.

Since a and b are digits, the only possible solution is a=3, b=7. Hence, Deborah is 37 and grandfather is 73 going on 74.

ABOUT THE AUTHOR

David J. Bodycombe was born in Darlington, England, in 1973. Over many years his creations have appeared in various TV and radio programmes, print media, board games, web sites, advertising campaigns and more.

He has contributed to numerous UK television shows including *Treasure Hunt* (BBC 2), *The Mole* (Channel 5), *Starfinder* (ITV), *Inside Clyde* (Disney) and five series of *The Crystal Maze* (Channel 4).

On BBC Radio 4 he appears on the problem solving show *Puzzle Panel*, and is also the researcher and question setter for the treasure hunt game *X Marks the Spot*.

David has authored many highly acclaimed puzzle books, and writes over 1000 puzzles a year for columns in periodicals such as the *Big Issue*, *Metro* and *Ireland on Sunday*.

After graduating in Mathematics from the University of Durham, David now runs Labyrinth Games, a games design consultancy, from his base in London.

Web site: www.labyrinthgames.com